STARS AND BEYOND

STORIES OF BLACK HEROES IN AVIATION

CASEY GRANT

Wasteland Press

www.wastelandpress.net
Shelbyville, KY USA

Stars and Beyond:
Stories of Black Heroes in Aviation
by Casey Grant

First Printing – June 2021
ISBN: 978-1-68111-412-5
Cover design idea by Casey Grant

Printed in the U.S.A.

0   1   2   3   4   5

ACKNOWLEDGEMENTS

In 2021 many Black women made astonishing contributions to the world. I will highlight a few that should be mentioned.

I would like to congratulate Kamala Harris for making history. She was sworn in as vice president of the United States on January 20, 2021, when Joe Biden was sworn in as the forty-seventh president. This made her the highest-ranking female official in United States history. She was the first female vice president, the first African American vice president, and the first Asian American vice president. She faced challenges but stayed strong and focused on what she could accomplish and what trails she could blaze so that those who come after her would find it easier to realize their dreams.

I would like to acknowledge Dr. Kizzmekia Corbett, an American viral immunologist at the Vaccine Research Center at the National Institute of Allergy and Infectious Diseases, National Institutes of Health based in Bethesda, Maryland. She has been central to the development of the COVID-19 Moderna mRNA vaccine, and Dr. Fauci credited her because "her work will have a substantial impact on ending the worst respiratory-disease pandemic in more than 100 years."

When Ohio Representative Marcia Fudge (1952-) took the oath as secretary of the Department of Housing and Urban Development in 2021, she became the first woman to serve as HUD secretary since 1979. She started her career as a lawyer, became mayor of Warrensville Heights, Ohio, in 1999, and took the oath of office in 2000. She won election to Congress in 2008. Marcia is a personal friend, and I wish her much success.

I thank all these women for their determination and accomplishments and for being an inspiration to all of us, particularly the little girls who look at what they have accomplished. They are stars in the sky and beyond, ones that light the way.

TABLE OF CONTENTS

INTRODUCTION

Do you dream of having a certain kind of career? Have you ever wanted to travel around the world or even further to outer space? Whatever it is, dream big! You can be a fighter pilot, space engineer, astronaut, flight attendant, commercial pilot, drone designer, even an aeronaut, a hot air balloon pilot. Aviation, which means flying, and aerospace, which means outer space, are both full of exciting careers.

This book introduces you to some Black pioneers in aviation and aerospace. You might have already heard of some of them, like Bessie Coleman or Mae C. Jemison, while others are a lot less famous.

Some of the most important events we will look at are the first Black pioneers in the sky, the way that African Americans formed their own flying clubs and schools when they could not join segregated ones, World Wars l and ll, the impact of the Civil Rights Movement, and the start of the Space Age. We will also look at the African American inventors who changed aviation and aerospace with their ideas.

My mission is to honor the legacy and the contributions of some Black pioneers in aviation. This book is dedicated to these heroes and to other African Americans who pursued their dreams, studied hard, and prepared themselves for their chosen dream careers. No matter what the obstacles were, they never gave up.

Most careers in aerospace and aviation require that you study hard in science and mathematics in grade school and study science, technology, engineering, or mathematics in a trade school, community college, or four-year college. To be a flight attendant, you need to learn first aid, how to work with people, and how to handle emergencies. Learning different languages is important if you want to travel internationally.

There are all kinds of programs to help you learn more about different careers in aviation and aerospace. The Federal Aviation Administration has a lot of resources on aviation careers at www.faa.gov/education/students/.

It also offers Aviation Career Academies with programs for students in grade school, middle school/junior high, and high school. [www.faa.gov/education/ace_academy/]

NASA has activities you can do to learn about aviation and aerospace at home. [www.nasa.gov/stem]

Talk to your teacher or if you are in a youth organization like Boys and Girls Clubs or scouting, ask your program leader about inviting someone who works in aviation or aerospace to speak to your school or program.

Another great source for Black achievements in all aspects of life is www.blackpast.org.

Enjoy the journey!

THE
PILOTS

BESSIE COLEMAN

Bessie Coleman was one of the most famous women of her day. She had two favorite sayings: "You've never lived till you've flown" and "I refused to take no for an answer." Her life was proof of these statements.

The photo is from Bessie Coleman's pilot's license.
Photo source: NASA/Creative Commons

Bessie Coleman, posing on the wheel of a Curtiss JN-4 "Jennie" airplane, is wearing a custom-designed flying suit. Photo credit: Smithsonian Institution.

Coleman was born on January 26, 1892, in Atlanta, Texas, to a family of sharecroppers, low-paid agricultural workers, and the tenth of thirteen children. Her mother was Black and her father was multiracial, Black and Native American. She wanted to attend college and saved all her money but could afford only one semester at the Colored Agricultural and Normal University (now Langston University) in Langston, Oklahoma.

During the Great Migration between 1916-1970, many African Americans moved from the South to the North, where there were more opportunities for jobs and less discrimination. Some of Coleman's brothers moved to Chicago, and in 1923 Coleman joined them. She attended Beauty Culture School and became a manicurist. Her brother John, who had fought in France during World War 1, told her war stories, including those about the military pilots. He also teased her that in France, women were allowed to enter aviation school.

She decided to learn to fly, but none of the United States schools where she applied accepted her because of her sex and race. Coleman refused to give up and decided to go to France to learn how to fly. To apply to schools in France and speak the language, when she got there, Coleman studied French at night.

At the barbershop where she worked, she met Robert S. Abbott, founder and publisher of *The Chicago Defender,* the most important Black-owned newspaper of its time and still published today digitally. Back then, it covered and campaigned mostly against violence toward Black people in the South and urged them to come to the North, where conditions were better.

Abbott and Jesse Binga, a local Black banker who founded a bank when other banks wouldn't lend to Black people, encouraged Coleman to pursue her dream career and even lent her the money to go to France, once a school accepted her. The Caudron Brothers' School of Aviation in Le Crotoy, France, accepted her application, and Coleman received her international pilot's license from the Fédération Aéronautique Internationale in Paris in 1921. This made her the first Black person to earn an international pilot's license.

When she returned to the United States, she became a stunt pilot at airshows, famous for her barnstorming tricks, such as flying upside down, swooping close to the ground, and then rising again at the last second. She became a sensation for her skills and courage. Newspapers called her "Queen Bess" and "Brave Bessie."

Coleman actively opposed discrimination and segregation and refused to perform for segregated audiences. Coleman even started saving money to open an aviation school that would admit both men and women of all races, but tragically, she died in 1926 when she fell from her plane while preparing for a show in Jacksonville, Florida.

The famous journalist and anti-lynching activist Ida B. Wells-Barnett addressed the crowd of mourners at Coleman's funeral service. She wasn't forgotten after her death. William J. Powell formed the Bessie Coleman Aero Club in Los Angeles in 1929 to honor her.

In 1931 John C. Robinson, Cornelius Coffey, Janet Bragg, and Willa Brown formed the Challenger Pilots' Association of Chicago, and in Robbins, Illinois, a group of Black pilots started an annual tradition of flying over her grave at Lincoln Cemetery in Alsip, Illinois, in tribute. Decades later in 1977, a group of African American women pilots named their association the Bessie Coleman Aviators Club in her honor.

In 1995 the United States issued a commemorative Bessie Coleman stamp. Finally, several streets have been named after her in the United States, mostly near airports and airfields.

CORNELIUS R. COFFEY

Cornelius Coffey (1903-1994) was born in Newport, Arkansas, where he took his first plane ride at an airshow when he was just thirteen. From then on, he wanted to be a pilot. He was rejected from every aviation school that he applied to because of his race, so instead he went to automotive school in Chicago. He and John C. Robinson, a fellow mechanic, met on the job and encouraged one another to fulfill their dreams of flying.

Photo source: National Air and Space Museum

He and Robinson applied to and were accepted by the Curtiss Wright School of Aviation. When they showed up for classes, the school tried to refuse them admission because of their race, but their employer, a white man named Emil Mack, threatened to sue the school if they were not admitted.

In the meantime, Robinson took a job as a janitor and listened to classes that way. When he was emptying the trash, he saw an advertisement for an airplane that pilots could build themselves. He and Coffey built this plane together and taught themselves to fly. The school was so impressed that they agreed to admit them on condition that they drop the lawsuit. Although they were not allowed to attend classes with white students, the school taught them at night. They graduated two years later, and Coffey received his commercial pilot's license in 1938.

He then opened his own aviation school, the Coffey School of Aeronautics at Harlem Airport on the South Side of Chicago. He and Robinson also opened the first U.S. Black-owned airport in Robbins, Illinois, when they were not allowed to open one in Chicago. Their aviation school's first class included two women, breaking yet another equality barrier. Between 1938 and 1945, more than 1,500 Black students attended, and many of them joined the Tuskegee Airmen. However, the school wasn't just for Black men. Coffey admitted both men and women and made sure that every class of ten students had at least one white student and one female student to prove that men and women and whites and Blacks could learn together.

When Italy invaded Ethiopia in 1935, Coffey and Robinson started training volunteer pilots to fight for Ethiopia's freedom. Ethiopia had defeated Italy in an earlier war and had never been colonized by a European country. Helping Ethiopia was especially important to them as Black men. Robinson went to Ethiopia in person to start making arrangements. He became commander of the Ethiopian Air Force, overseeing a fleet of twenty. He earned the nickname "the brown condor" for his flying. He narrowly escaped being captured and had to leave when Italy defeated Ethiopia in 1936.

John C. Robinson with one of the planes he flew during the fight for Ethiopia's independence. Photo source: National Air and Space Museum.

In 1939 Coffey, his wife Willa Brown, and Enoch P. Waters (editor of *The Chicago Defender*), opened the National Negro Airmen's Association of America to help encourage Black interest in aviation. (Back then, "Negro" was the preferred term.) They later changed the name to indicate that membership was open to all, but they still focused on encouraging Black people to consider aviation careers.

The association organized events like an airshow and a public air tour to finish in Washington, D.C. where the pilots would meet with politicians to try to convince them to open the Army Air Corps to

Blacks. Dale White and Chauncey Spencer, the two pilots, met with Senator Harry S. Truman and Representative Everett Dirksen, who both agreed to help.

Once the war was over, Coffey went back to school at the Lewis School of Aeronautics in Lockport, Illinois, to study the new advances in aviation, and he stayed to teach there and at other schools. He retired from teaching in 1969 but kept working in aviation for the rest of his life.

Willa Brown was herself a pioneer. Her mother was Black, and her father was Native American. She was the first Black woman to earn a pilot's license in the United States in 1939, the first woman to earn both a pilot's and a mechanic's license, and the first Black officer in the Civil Air Patrol. She advocated for the United States military to include Blacks in pilot training, and she taught many of the future Tuskegee instructors and airmen. Brown was also the first African American woman to run for Congress.

Willa Brown
Photo source: National Air and Space Museum

WILLIAM J. POWELL

Like many people in this book, William J. Powell (1897-1942) and his family were born in the South but moved north to Chicago when he was young so that he and his brothers and sisters could receive a good education. He went to the University of Illinois' electrical engineering program but volunteered to join the military when World War I broke out. Powell was injured in a poison gas attack, and like many World War I veterans who had been exposed to poison gas, it affected his health for the rest of his life, but he did recover enough to return to school.

Photo credit: National Air and Space Museum, Smithsonian Institution

After he graduated, he opened several auto parts shops and gas stations in Chicago. When he went to an Army reunion in Paris, he tried flying for the first time. He decided that he wanted to be a pilot. He applied to several aviation schools, including the Army Air Corps, but all of them rejected him until he finally applied to and was accepted at the Los Angeles School of Flight, which took students of all races from around the world.

Powell sold his businesses and moved with his family to California. He didn't want to fly just because he loved it. He saw that aviation was a growing industry and thought that Black Americans could find jobs in aviation.

He started a club in 1929, naming it the Bessie Coleman Aero Club to honor her and keep her memory alive after her death in 1936. His opened his club to people of all races and to both men and women, as you can see in the photograph of some club members. Powell is the man standing on the far right.

Photo credit: National Air and Space Museum, Smithsonian Institution

Powell organized an all-Black airshow in 1931, which drew 15,000 attendees. He also opened the Bessie Coleman Flying school, published a magazine about Black Americans in aviation, and founded the Bessie Coleman Aero Company, the first airplane manufacturer owned by an African American.

Powell wrote a book, *Black Wings*, a novel very closely based on his own life. He gave the book that title because he wanted to see young Black people "fill the air with black wings," not just as pilots, but as engineers, mechanics, manufacturers, and aviation business owners. As you can see, he dedicated his book to Bessie Coleman.

Photo credit: Smithsonian Institution

Powell died in 1942 when he was only forty-five years old. Many other WWI veterans who had been exposed to poison gas died young as well, even after surviving the war. Today, chemical weapons are banned.

CHARLES ALFRED ANDERSON

Charles Alfred Anderson became fascinated by planes at a young age and dreamed of being a pilot. He applied to pilot schools but was rejected because of his race. He decided to make his dream come true another way and attended mechanics classes and "ground school" where people learned to maintain airstrips and airfields. This brought him close enough to pilots that he could watch, ask questions, and learn.

Charles Alfred Anderson and First Lady Eleanor Roosevelt
Photo source: United States Air Force.

He finally realized that if he wanted to learn enough to fly, he would have to buy his own plane. He borrowed from friends and family, bought a small used plane, and taught himself, based on what he had observed and learned from others. Anderson joined a small flying club and made friends with a pilot who didn't own a plane. They made a deal that the pilot would teach Anderson, in exchange for renting his plane on weekends to visit his mother in Atlantic City.

He learned enough that he could finally get his own license in 1929. He tried to get an air transport license that would let him fly more than a small private plane but was rejected because of his race. However, Ernest Buehl, a German pilot who had been invited to the United States to help establish an airmail service, intervened, and Anderson received his air transport license in 1932, the first African American to do so.

Dr. Albert Forsythe, a Black pilot and physician, heard of this accomplishment and reached out to Anderson to suggest that they work together to get more African Americans involved in aviation. To generate publicity and to show that it could be done, in 1933 they became the first African Americans to fly a transcontinental round trip from Atlantic City, New Jersey, to Los Angeles, and back. They also embarked on a tour of North, Central, and South America in 1934 on a plane named The Booker T. Washington.

In 1938 Howard University hired Anderson to start a Civilian Pilot Training Program, and in 1940 Tuskegee Institute hired him to train African American aviators to fight during WWII. First Lady Eleanor Roosevelt visited Tuskegee in 1941 to learn more about its polio research. (The world was experiencing pandemic polio, a serious disease that killed or paralyzed thousands of people, especially children.) She had heard of Anderson's work and asked to meet him. She said that people had told her that Blacks could not be pilots, but he was proving that they could. He invited her to take a flight with him so she could experience it in person. This helped build momentum for training more Black pilots as part of the existing Civilian Pilot Training Program.

Tuskegee named Anderson the ground commander and chief instructor for the 99th Pursuit Squadron, the first African American fighter squadron. People nicknamed him "Chief" and called him that for the rest of his life. This squadron and three others combined to create the 332nd Fighter Group, the famous Tuskegee Airmen.

JAMES BANNING

James Banning (1900-1933) grew up on his parents' farm in Canton, Oklahoma, and went to elementary school in a schoolhouse they built on their property to make sure he would get an education. He went on to study electrical engineering at Iowa State College in Ames, Iowa, and took his first airplane ride in 1920 at a performing air show. This made him want to fly, but flight schools wouldn't admit him because of his race.

Photo source: National Air and Space Museum

He decided to start his own business, the J. H. Banning Auto Repair Shop, but at the same time, he studied privately with a World War I aviator at Raymond Fisher's Flying Field in Des Moines, Iowa.

Banning earned his mechanic's certificate and private pilot's license in 1926. Nobody would sell him a plane, so he bought a plane that had been sold for scrap, repaired it, and named it Miss Ames because he liked Iowa State College and Ames, Iowa, so much.

In 1929 when the Bessie Coleman Aero Club Aviation School for African Americans opened in Los Angeles, William Powell asked Banning to teach there, so he left his home and business to help other Black Americans learn how to fly. Powell staged the first all-Black air show in 1931, the All-Negro Air Show. More than 15,000 people paid to attend and even more watched from their homes. That convinced Powell, Banning, and others that people wanted to watch and applaud Black aviators.

In 1932 Banning and Thomas Cox Allen, a mechanic, became the first Black Americans to fly coast to coast. The flight time was forty-two hours, but they made the trip over twenty-one days, leaving Los Angeles on September 18, 1932, and arriving at Long Island, New York, on October 9, 1932. Their plane, like Miss Ames, had been assembled from pieces, and they were worried about crashes, but they were more determined to show the world what Black pilots could do.

Banning and Allen had a great idea for raising funds. Each time they stopped, they invited people to contribute toward their expenses: gas, food, shelter, aircraft repairs. They called themselves the Flying Hobos. (A hobo is someone without a job, who goes from town to town, looking for work and asking for food and shelter if they could not find work.)

In exchange, Banning and Allen invited local donors to sign their names in *The Gold Book*, which the pilots had dubbed the lower left wingtip of the aircraft. This way, the people who helped them could feel like they were part of history, too.

The two men did not have the equipment or money to fly nonstop and had to fly an indirect route so they could stop in places where they knew people and where Blacks would be welcome. Sometimes, they were flying in weather that was so bad that they couldn't even see the ends of the wings, and other times, they had to land among strangers.

They didn't publicize the flight at all, so imagine how surprised some farmers were to see an airplane coming to land on a rural road or in an empty field and see the Black pilot and machinist get out and ask where they could buy gas. However, word of mouth traveled, and eventually the press started to cover their trip. Sometimes, they would arrive to find a crowd waiting for them.

When they arrived in New York, Mayor Jimmy Walker gave them a key to the city in a ceremony to welcome them. The Cotton Club in Harlem, probably the world's most famous jazz club in the world, celebrated their accomplishment with performances by Duke Ellington and Cab Calloway.

Banning was killed in a plane crash at an air show in San Diego, California, on February 5, 1933. Because of his race, he hadn't been allowed to fly a plane in the air show but had to be a passenger. He had more extensive experience and was far more qualified than the aviation machinist who flew the plane.

EUGENE J. BULLARD

Eugene Bullard (1895-1961) was the first African American military pilot to fly in combat and the only African American pilot in World War I. It is also possible that he was the first Black fighter pilot in the world.

He was born in Georgia and ran away from home when he was just eleven and worked various jobs to support himself. When he was seventeen, he left the United States for Europe where Black people had much more freedom. He decided to live in France, saying later, "It seemed to me that French democracy influenced the minds of both black and white Americans there and helped us all act like brothers."

He didn't start flying until after he had joined the French military's famous Foreign Legion during World War I. After being wounded, he bet a friend $2,000 that he could join the French aviation forces, and he won that bet. In 1916 he entered the Aéronautique Militaire, the French equivalent of the air force.

Not many records from his time still exist, but he claimed two victories in air fights. He was such a good flyer that other pilots nicknamed him "the black swallow of death." (Swallows are known for their flying agility, a skill that fighter pilots also needed.) Stories from the time describe how he added an insignia to his airplane, showing a heart with a dagger running through it and the slogan "All Blood Runs Red." He sometimes flew with a pet rhesus monkey that he called Jimmy.

Eugene Bullard and his monkey, Jimmy
Photo source: Smithsonian Institution

When the United States entered the war in 1917, Bullard tried to join the United States Air Force but was rejected, officially because of bureaucratic requirements but really because of his race. The Aéronautique Militaire later removed Bullard. The reasons why are lost, but most stories say that he had a confrontation with a superior officer, though some say that the United States government was embarrassed that an African American was flying for France because his own country wouldn't let him fly, and they urged the French to remove him.

Bullard returned to the Foreign Legion, and after the war, he started a nightclub, Le Grand Duc (The Grand Duke) and an American-style bar, L'Escadrille, a now outdated term for a squad of airplanes. He became friends with many American celebrities in France, including authors Langston Hughes and F. Scott Fitzgerald, musician Louis Armstrong, and dancer Josephine Baker.

When the Nazis took over Germany, Bullard became worried for France. He started to spy for the French government on Nazi sympathizers in France who were working for Germany to invade France. His bar and nightclub were some of the best in Paris, and German officers often went to them. Many Germans believed that Blacks weren't intelligent enough to understand German, and Bullard hid the fact that he could understand it very well, so he was able to eavesdrop on them very easily.

When Germany invaded France, Bullard enrolled again in the military, this time as a machine gunner, and was again wounded. He finally returned to the United States, but France didn't forget his service. In 1954 they chose him to be one of three men to relight the flame at the Tomb of the Known Soldier in Paris, and in 1959 he received his fifteenth medal from France when they made him a knight of the Legion of Honor, the highest medal and recognition that the French government can give.

When he returned to the United States, he took up various jobs. When he attended a Paul Robeson concert, a mob that included police officers beat several of the attendees, including Bullard. Paul Robeson was a Black bass-baritone who became famous not only for his singing but for his cultural achievements and activism in such causes as the Civil Rights Movement.

It took decades for the United States to recognize Bullard's contributions. The Georgia Aviation Hall of Fame admitted him in 1989, and in 1994 posthumously, he received a commission as second lieutenant in the Air Force.

In 2019 the 125th anniversary of his birth, the Museum of Aviation in Georgia erected a statue of Bullard. Attending the unveiling were members of Tuskegee Airmen and official representatives of the United States and French militaries.

Photo source: Milliyet. Public domain

Ahmet Ali Çelikten (1883-1969) might have been the first Black fighter pilot in the world. If he was the first, he started flying only months before Bullard did.

Çelikten was born in Izmir, Turkey, part of the Ottoman Empire, and his parents were Black, Arab, and Turkish. His last name is pronounced *Chel EEK ten.*

He first joined the Ottoman Empire's Navy as a lieutenant, but when the Empire saw how important aviation was going to be in World War I, he went to naval flight school in 1914 and graduated in 1916, before Eugene Bullard did.

While the United States didn't recognize Bullard's achievements for decades, Çelikten received several promotions for his courage and skill and became a captain. After the war ended, he remained active in aviation, fighting in the Turkish War of Independence and later serving in the Turkish Air Force.

JANET HARMON
WATERFORD BRAGG

Janet Bragg (1907-1993) was the first Black American woman to earn a commercial pilot's license which authorizes a pilot to fly a bigger plane than a private pilot's license does, a bit like the difference between a driver's license and a trucker's license.

Bragg had always been interested in learning how to fly, but instead, she studied nursing. Like many of the first African American pilots, Bragg left the South, where she was born, to come to Chicago during the Great Migration. She became the only woman in her class at Curtiss Wright Aeronautical School in Chicago where Cornelius Coffey and John C. Robinson taught. However, most of her fellow students refused to help her or socialize with her because they thought that only men should fly.

She persisted in her studies, and Coffey and Robinson encouraged her. Because she didn't give up her job as a nurse, she was one of the few students who was earning money and actually spending her earnings on a plane for the school. She also helped pay to construct an airfield in Robbins, Illinois. She, Coffey, Robinson, Willa Brown, and a few other classmates formed the Challenge Air Pilots Association.

She enrolled in the Civilian Pilot Training Program at Tuskegee Institute in Tuskegee, Alabama, and earned her commercial pilot's license in 1943. She passed the test, but the examiner refused to certify a Black woman, so she had to take the examination again at the Pal-Waukee Airport near Chicago, where they did give her the license she had earned. Bragg wrote a book about her life, *Soaring Above Setbacks: The Autobiography of Janet Harmon Bragg, African American Aviator.*

Photo credit: Smithsonian Institution - Janet Bragg

MARLON DEWITT GREEN and DAVID HARRIS

Marlon DeWitt Green (1929-2009) joined the U.S. Air Force as a young man. He first hoped to become an airline mechanic but then decided to become a pilot. He was accepted into pilot training school in 1950 and trained in the same class as Virgil "Gus" Grissom, one of the famous Mercury 7 astronauts.

Photo source: United States Air Force. Marlon Green

While on leave in 1957, Green applied for a job with Continental Airlines but left the application blank where it asked about his race. He also did not attach a photograph. He was accepted but when Continental found out that he was Black, they turned him down, although at the same time, they accepted five other white pilots who had less flying experience.

Green filed a complaint with the Colorado Anti-Discrimination Commission, and he and the Commission took the case all the way to the Supreme Court. U.S. Attorney General Robert Kennedy was one of the people who supported Green. The Supreme Court's rulings are final. It took six years, but Green won. Continental hired him in 1963, and he first flew for them in 1965. Because the court case against Continental Airlines took so long, Green was not the first African American commercial pilot in the United States.

American Airlines hired Captain David Harris in 1964, so technically, he became the first African American commercial pilot. (New York Airways had hired Perry Young, a former instructor at Tuskegee, as a helicopter pilot in 1957.)

Harris (1934-) did not grow up with any special interest in flying. In an interview, he said that perhaps this was because there weren't any visible Black pilots for him to admire. "World War II and the Tuskegee Airmen had come and gone, and [Black pilots] were not accepted and therefore not seen in the commercial arena," he said in an interview.

He joined the ROTC in high school and then the U.S. Air Force in 1958. He completed his tour of duty in 1964, and American Airlines hired him that same year. During his phone interview, he told the pilot interviewing him that he was Black, and the pilot replied that the only thing American Airlines cared about was his ability to fly. Harris retired in 1994, thirty years later. Other commercial airlines started hiring Black pilots around that time. The full list appears at the end of this book.

Photo source: National Air and Space Museum
David Harris talking with a group of young people about being a pilot

LESLIE IRBY

As a child, Leslie Irby first wanted to be an Olympic athlete, but when she heard Bessie Coleman's story, she decided that she wanted to be a pilot like her. Irby flew for the first time when she was sixteen years old through a program from the Organization of Black Aerospace Professionals (OBAP). The program gives Black children and teens the chance to learn about aviation as a career.

Only seven years later, she was in a car accident that left most of her body paralyzed. When she learned that she would need to use a wheelchair for the rest of her life, she asked if they had a pink wheelchair. She was determined not to let the accident and her paralysis change her attitude or her dream. She found a program called Able Flight that helps people with disabilities become pilots and enrolled in Able Flight at Purdue University. Irby graduated in 2019 with a license as a sports pilot, the first African American female pilot who uses a wheelchair.

Irby and others with similar disabilities flew the Sky Arrow 600 aircraft, a light sport plane equipped with hand controls.

Irby is an inspiration to others not to give up and a reminder that a dream deferred doesn't have to be a dream denied. She says her "wheelchair is my blessing," and she has some more rockin' n' rollin' to do."

BILL COSTEN

Bill Costen (1947-) is another kind of pilot, a balloon pilot. Balloon pilots are also called aeronauts. He did not plan on becoming a balloonist, let alone the first African American one, but he saw it as an opportunity when he became aware of the option.

Photo source: Hartford Courant
Bill Costen with items from his collection

After he graduated from college with a double major in mathematics and psychology, the Buffalo Bills drafted him, but he played only a few preseason games before the team cut him. The team traded him to their minor league team based in Hartford.

When he was in Hartford, planning to work in the insurance industry, a cousin invited him to join him and four other friends to start a ballooning club. He agreed, and in 1975, he designed his own balloon, The State of Connecticut Bicentennial Balloon, and started his own company, Sky Endeavors. He was one of the very first Black aeronauts and the first Black person to earn a commercial aeronaut's license.

Photo source: Bill Costen www.skyendeavors.net

He is also an active photographer and collects African American memorabilia, items from history, as a way to celebrate Black history. He founded the Costen Cultural Exhibition, a traveling exhibit that includes artifacts from the Tuskegee Airmen, items from Black golfing history, and books by Black authors. You can see items from the collection at www.skyendeavors.net.

In 2016 the Balloon Federation of America named him an Ed Yost Master Pilot, an award named for its founder. His daughter, Chantal Potter, made *Balloon Man*, a documentary about him, in 2020.

THE ASTRONOMERS AND ASTRONAUTS

ROBERT HENRY LAWRENCE

Robert Henry Lawrence (1935-1967) was selected for the United States space program and would have been the first African American astronaut if it weren't for his untimely death. He excelled in school and graduated from high school when he was only twenty. He went to Bradley College, where he majored in chemistry.

Lawrence joined the Air Force Reserve Officers' Training Corps (ROTC) and became a pilot when he was twenty-one. He flew several test flights that launched unpowered spacecraft so that the Air Force and NASA could learn more about how objects returning from space would re-enter the Earth's atmosphere. NASA credited him for collecting data that helped them develop the space shuttle.

Photo source: United States Air Force

He joined the Air Force Test Pilot School in 1967, received a promotion to major, and was selected for the astronaut training program. He was scheduled to go onto the Manned Orbital Laboratory (MOL) and would have been the first United States' first Black astronaut.

However, he died in a flight accident in late 1967 when a student he was training crashed the plane. In 1997 his name was added to the Space Mirror Memorial at the Kennedy Space Center in Florida, which honors all the astronauts who died in the performance of their duties.

Lawrence with other members of the MOL program: Lt. Col. Robert T. Herres, Maj. Donald H. Peterson and Maj. James A. Abrahamson
Photo credit: United States Air Force

At the time of Lawrence's death, the Air Force didn't consider anybody an astronaut unless they had actually flown into space, but the Astronaut Memorial Foundation, which funded and manages the memorial, successfully asked the Air Force to designate him an astronaut so they could add him to the memorial.

The Space Mirror Memorial that honors Lawrence and
other astronauts who died in the line of duty
Photo source: NASA

Another Black aviator, Captain Edward J. Dwight Jr., entered training in the early 1960s before Lawrence did. His first dream was to be an artist, and he said in an interview, "I had a library card at 4, and soon I was studying the great masters such as Leonardo da Vinci and Michelangelo." However, his father advised him to pursue engineering instead, since it was easier to find engineering jobs.

Dwight joined the U.S. Air Force, graduated with a degree in aeronautical engineering in 1957, and joined a test pilot program. He started astronaut training but was not selected for the second phase of the program. After Dwight left the military, he pursued his first love, art, and became a sculptor.

BERNARD A. HARRIS JR.

Bernard A Harris (1956-) is a doctor, an astronaut, and an entrepreneur. (Someone who starts or funds new businesses is called an entrepreneur.) Harris was the first Black American to perform an extra-vehicular activity (EVA), popularly known as spacewalk. Spacewalks are exciting because they let astronauts look directly into space in any direction, with nothing but a spacesuit between them and outer space. Sometimes astronauts need to perform maintenance on a vehicle from the outside, while other times, they perform scientific experiments during spacewalks.

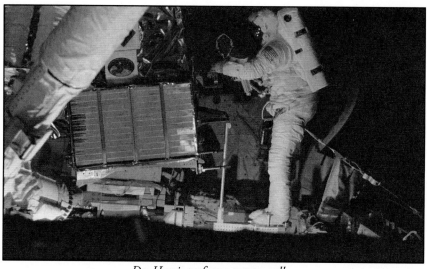

Dr. Harris performs a spacewalk.
Photo source: NASA

Harris loved science, including space exploration, from an early age and regularly participated in science fairs. He first wanted to be a doctor and earned an undergraduate degree in biology before going to medical school. In 1987 he went to Ames Research Center, part of NASA, to study muscles and what happens when they go unused or underused. This is a very important topic for astronauts because in outer space, gravity is not as strong as it is on Earth. This means that astronauts do not use their muscles as much as people on Earth do, and this can cause physical problems for them. The next year, he went to Brooks Air Force Base in San Antonio, Texas, to study flight surgery. He then returned to Ames to study the effects that being in outer space have on the human body.

Dr. Harris and another astronaut, Michael Foale, prepare for their spacewalk.
Photo source: NASA

In 1990 NASA selected him to join an astronaut program which began in 1991. He first went into outer space in 1993. He returned to space in 1995, when he performed his first spacewalk. He retired from

NASA in 1996 but remained very active in promoting science and space exploration and in developing new technology.

He currently serves as CEO of the National Math and Science Initiative, a nonprofit that helps young people learn science and technology, and he is the president and CEO of Vesalius Ventures, Inc. Vesalius is named after Andreas Vesalius, the man whom many people consider the first anatomist or person to scientifically study the human body, back in the 1500s. Vesalius Ventures develops new medical technologies.

BENJAMIN BANNEKER

Benjamin Banneker (1731-1806) taught himself mathematics, writing, and astronomy. He was one of the earliest American racial activists as well as the first Black American astronomer. His parents were farmers who valued education. His grandmother and mother taught him to read, and his parents sent him to a Quaker school that accepted Black students, even though he could attend only for a very short time.

Banneker invented an irrigation system for the family farm and built an accurate clock out of wood, even though he had never seen a clock before, just a pocket watch. Clocks were so rare then that people came from miles around to see his clock.

Photo credit: United States Postal Service

A rich neighbor, George Ellicott, learned about how talented Banneker was and how much he wanted to learn, so he loaned him books on astronomy and math and astronomical instruments. Ellicott was a Quaker, and most Quakers believed in racial equality and providing education to people of all races. Banneker read all the books he could about every topic.

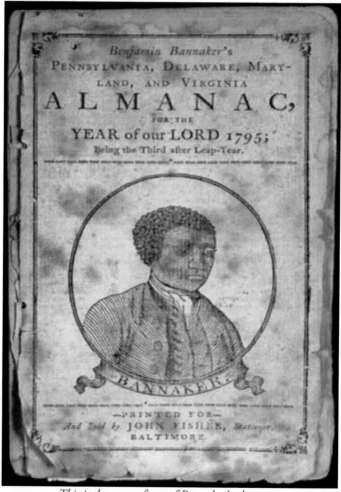

This is the cover of one of Banneker's almanacs.
Photo credit: Library of Congress.

George Ellicott recommended Banneker to his cousin, Andrew Ellicott, who was surveying the territory for building Washington D.C. as the nation's capital. In 1792 he wrote his own almanacs, which are books to help farmers and businessmen predict the weather and learn other important information. For farmers, a good almanac can mean the difference between crops dying and crops living.

Banneker's almanac featured information about astronomy, including when tides would be high or low (the moon causes tides) and when to expect lunar or solar eclipses (an eclipse is when light from the sun or moon is blocked). This work earned him the nickname "the sable astronomer." (Sable means black.)

He also wrote to Thomas Jefferson, urging him to think of and treat Black people as equals. He even succeeded in persuading Jefferson that the reason many Black people were not as successful as white people was because Black people did not have equal access to education and other opportunities, rather than not being as hard-working or intelligent. Jefferson sent a copy of Banneker's almanac to the Royal Academy of Sciences in Paris as proof of how much Black people could accomplish.

CHARLES W. CHAPELLE

Charles W. Chapelle (1872-1941) was what people sometimes call a Renaissance man, somebody who excels in very different areas. He was the first African American to invent a new kind of airplane; the first main electrician at U.S. Steel, one of the biggest and most important companies in the world then; one of the earliest Black architects in the United States; and founder of a major business importing goods from Africa to the United States, although it failed just as the Great Depression began.

Photo source: Morris Brown College. Public domain

Chapelle was excited when the Wright brothers successfully invented the first airplane. However, their airplane could fly only short distances, and he knew that airplanes would need to fly longer distances before they could revolutionize travel and transportation.

At the First Industrial Aero Show in 1911 in New York, Chapelle exhibited the plane that he had invented that could safely fly long distance flights. He was the only Black exhibitor at the show. Chapelle won a medal for this design, and his plane went on show at the United States Aeronautical Reserve, one of the earliest aviation organizations and the most important of its time, based at Harvard University.

KATHERINE JOHNSON and VANCE H. MARCHBANKS

Katherine Johnson (1918-2020) was one of the inspirations of the book *Hidden Figures*, which later became a movie. She was a brilliant student, especially at math, and skipped several grades in school. She attended West Virginia State College, where one of her professors developed a new class for her, since their existing classes were not hard enough to challenge her.

Photo source: NASA

After she graduated, she taught and then took some time to start a family. She and her husband heard about the West Area Computing section at the National Advisory Committee for Aeronautics (the organization that eventually became NASA), which was staffed entirely by Black people.

They moved to Virginia, and she worked there in 1953. Back then, there were thousands of math problems that had to be solved to launch a spacecraft, and without many reliable computers, people did the math themselves. They had to be incredibly accurate because so much depended on being correct. Her work was instrumental in planning the United States' first flight into space with a human being on board.

One of the first astronauts, John Glenn, said that he would fly on a mission only if Johnson's calculations agreed with the computers' calculations, since he trusted her more. She retired from NASA in 1986. President Obama gave her the Presidential Medal of Freedom Award, the highest honor that the government can give to a civilian. Johnson used to say, "I loved going to work every single day."

When she died at the age of 101, NASA Administrator Jim Bridenstine said, "Ms. Johnson helped our nation enlarge the frontiers of space even as she made huge strides that also opened doors for women and people of color in the universal human quest to explore space. Her dedication and skill as a mathematician helped put humans on the moon and before that made it possible for our astronauts to take the first steps in space that we now follow on a journey to Mars."

Most of Johnson's colleagues were also Black women. One of them, Mary Jackson, was NASA's first Black female engineer. Mary Jackson (1921-2005) started at NACA in 1951. Her supervisor, Kazimierz Czarnecki, a Polish immigrant and engineer, urged her to study engineering. The closest engineering school was still segregated, and so she needed to get special permission to attend classes. In 1958 after NACA became NASA, she became NASA's first Black female engineer. In 2020 NASA renamed their headquarters in Washington D.C. the Mary W. Black Headquarters.

Dorothy Vaughan was NACA's first Black supervisor. Vaughan left her job as a math teacher in 1943 to join NACA, and in 1949, she received a promotion to lead the West Area Computing team. In 1958 NACA became NASA, and Vaughan and many of the members of the West Area Computing section joined its desegregated replacement, the Analysis and Computation Division (ACD).

Another pioneer is Dr. Vance Marchbanks who made it possible for the United States to send humans into space. During John Glenn's historic first flight in space, Dr. Marchbanks monitored his heart and other vital signs to understand how space flight affects the human body.

From his earliest days, Marchbanks wanted to be a doctor. As a boy, he would "operate" on cherries from the tree in his backyard, cutting them open, removing the seeds, and sewing the cherries back together. After he graduated from medical school, he started to work at a veterans hospital. There he met Benjamin O. Davis Jr.

When World War II started, Marchbanks became a flight surgeon. In addition to treating pilots, he also looked for ways to keep pilots safe, and he designed a new oxygen mask tester. He won a commendation for that and for developing a system to measure the effects of high-altitude flights (flying at great heights).

Marchbanks retired from the Air Force and started to work on the United States space program as head physician for the Mercury space program that would send humans into space.

He was posted to a tracking station in Nigeria, and when he learned that the local medical library did not have enough books, he wrote to doctors he knew and to medical publishers and encouraged them to send more than 200 books.

Photo source: United States Department of Defense

After he retired from government work, he worked for a company that developed technology for the space program. He oversaw the medical testing of the moon suit and backpack that astronauts would use.

Dr. Marchbanks contributed in another way to opening the skies for Black pilots and astronauts. He studied people with the gene for sickle cell anemia and learned that not everybody with the gene actually develops sickle cell anemia. Sickle cell anemia is a serious disease that mostly affects Black people and people from the Mediterranean region. It is an inherited condition, and because flying can make the symptoms much worse and even kill people who have it, the Air Force did not let anybody who carried the gene for sickle cell anemia become a pilot. Dr. Marchbanks' research convinced the U.S. Air Force to allow people with the sickle cell gene but not the disease itself to become pilots.

CHARLES F. BOLDEN JR.

Charles Bolden (1946-) became the first Black permanent administrator at NASA. He applied to the United States Naval Academy when he was in high school. However, because Bolden was from South Carolina, Senator Strom Thurmond, who believed in segregation, was one of the people who decided whether the Academy would consider Bolden and blocked his application. Bolden wrote to President Johnson who intervened so that Bolden's application would be considered fairly.

Photo source: NASA

Bolden excelled at the Academy and became a naval aviator. During the Vietnam War, he flew more than 100 missions. When he returned to the United States, he continued his military career and became a test pilot in 1979.

In 1980, NASA selected him as an astronaut, and Bolden went into space on several missions. After the space shuttle Challenger exploded in 1986, killing all seven aboard, Bolden became chief of the Safety Division at the Johnson Space Center to create new rules and requirements to ensure that there would not be any more disasters like that. Bolden was inducted into the U.S. Astronaut Hall of Fame in 2006.

In 2009 President Obama appointed him to be the NASA administrator. During an interview, Bolden said that President Obama gave him three priorities: to inspire children to enter science and math careers, to help NASA develop more international relationships, and to reach out to the Muslim world to "help them feel good about their historic contribution to science." While he was administrator, NASA landed its first rover on Mars.

Bolden once said, "Always do your best in whatever you do; set goals and seek challenges; become a role model for those coming behind you; and always have God in your heart."

LELAND MELVIN

Leland Melvin (1964-) is the first NFL player to go into space. As a child, he loved science and planned to become a scientist or engineer. He received a football scholarship to the University of Richmond and twice earned recognition as an Honorable Mention All-American football player. The Detroit Lions drafted Melvin in 1986, but when he injured his hamstring during training, they cut him.

Photo source: NASA

Melvin went to graduate school at the University of Virginia, and the Dallas Cowboys recruited him in 1987. He didn't want to delay his education, so he arranged for the university to give him recorded lectures that he could study while at training camp. That didn't leave him much time off, and some of his teammates made fun of him for not partying; some of them even called him a nerd. Melvin didn't let the teasing bother him. However, he injured his hamstring again during training, so he decided to leave football and finish his degree in material science engineering.

He started as an engineer at NASA in 1989, and in 1998 after a friend talked him into applying to the astronaut program, he began astronaut training at the Johnson Space Center in Texas. He was in an accident during training, and the accident left him completely deaf for weeks, although he regained some hearing in his right ear. Because of the damage to his ears, he thought he would never be able to go into space.

Melvin started working as an educator for NASA, encouraging young people to think about a career in science or technology. Then he received medical clearance from a doctor who said that he would not hurt his ears by going into space, and he flew two missions. About his time in space, he said, "I thought about all the places on Earth where there's unrest and war, and here we were flying above all that, working together as one team to help advance our civilization."

After that, he returned to work for NASA's education department and wrote a book, *Chasing Space: An Astronaut's Story of Grit, Grace, and Second Chances*. He often talks about how he faced times when he thought he would have to let go of a dream and says, "We have setbacks and we have comebacks."

GUION (GUY) BLUFORD

Guy Bluford (1942-) was the first African American in space and the second person of African descent to go to space. He is a retired U.S. Air Force officer and fighter pilot and a former NASA astronaut.

Photo source: NASA

One of his first hobbies was building model airplanes. When he was in school, he dreamed of a career in aerospace and went to Pennsylvania State University to earn a degree in aerospace engineering. After that, he joined the Air Force and earned a master's degree and a doctorate in aerospace engineering.

Bluford earned three college degrees in space engineering, which teaches people how to build and fly spaceships. He flew four trips into outer space. After leaving NASA, he worked in the aviation industry as a senior aerospace engineering executive and eventually started his own consulting firm.

There were three Black people in the training class of 1978. Bluford was one of them; the other two were Fred Gregory and Ron McNair. Bluford said that he was selected for the program because he had experience as a pilot and as an engineer.

While he did not set out to be the first Black American in space, he is proud of his accomplishment and the role he played in history. "I wanted to set the standard, do the best job possible, so that other people would be comfortable with African-Americans flying in space and African-Americans would be proud of being participants in the space program and...encourage others to do the same."

Like many Black aviation pioneers, there are schools named after him to honor his achievements, but there is also a more unusual one. In 2017 the Mann Center for the Performing Arts hired Black composer Nolan Williams Jr. to write a musical piece called "Hold Fast to Dreams" for orchestra and choir to honor Bluford.

MAE C. JEMISON

Mae Carol Jemison (1956-) was born in Alabama, but when she was very young, her parents moved to Chicago so she and her brother and sister could get a good education. Her parents encouraged her to follow her interest in science and technology, and when she was just sixteen, she went to Stanford University, one of the best schools in the world, where she majored in chemical engineering and African American studies.

Photo source: NASA

She went to Cornell University to become a doctor and worked for two years in the Peace Corps, a program that sends Americans to other countries to help them in medicine, agriculture, technology, or other projects. She went to West Africa where she helped manage healthcare. When she came back to the United States, she worked as a doctor.

Jemison then decided that she wanted to become an astronaut. She applied to the program and was one of only 15 people selected from 2,000 applicants. She became the first African American woman in space in 1992, when she was assigned to a biology mission on Spacelab, a science laboratory attached to the space shuttle. During her eight days in space, she performed biology and medical experiments.

Astronauts are not allowed to bring many things with them into space due to limited room and because every ounce counts. However, Jemison brought a portrait of Bessie Coleman with her to pay tribute to the woman who had inspired her.

Later on, Jemison taught at Dartmouth College and started her own technology company, the Jemison Group. She is also a public speaker who encourages people to get a good education so they can follow their dreams.

In an interview, she said, "What we find is that if you have a goal that is very, very far out, and you approach it in little steps, you start to get there faster. Your mind opens up to the possibilities."

NEIL DEGRASSE TYSON

Neil deGrasse Tyson is probably America's most famous astronomer today and maybe the most famous American astronomer ever. He studies astrophysics which is about the physics of outer space, such as planets and stars. As an astronomer, he thinks it is very important to teach people of all ages about astronomy and space exploration.

Photo source: NASA Goddard Space Center

To help educate the public, he's written fifteen books (so far) and has hosted many different television shows about astronomy and outer space. Tyson believes that science teaches many important lessons, including that "We are all connected. To each other, biologically. To the earth, chemically. To the rest of the universe, atomically."

He also believes that every day, people should try to learn something new. "Whether or not you can never become great at something, you can always become better at it. Don't ever forget that! And don't say 'I'll never be good.' You can become better! And one day you'll wake up and you'll find out how good you actually became."

Tyson grew up in New York City and when he was nine, he went to the Hayden Planetarium's sky theater show. From then on, he knew that he wanted to be an astronomer. He credits Dr. Mark Chartrand III, the director of the planetarium, for helping to spark his interest in astronomy by the way that he communicated about science, making it exciting and understandable. The Hayden Planetarium is part of the American Museum of Natural History, and Tyson eventually became its director.

He attended the Bronx High School of Science, one of the most prestigious high schools in the country, which attracts some of the most promising and hard-working students in the city.

He applied to Cornell University, where the famous astronomer Carl Sagan was teaching at the time. The admissions committee – the people who review college applications – was so impressed by his application that they forwarded his application to Sagan. He invited Tyson to visit Cornell for the day, and when Tyson wasn't sure if he could catch a bus back that night, Sagan offered to let him stay with his family. Tyson later said that he knew early on that he wanted to be a scientist, but he learned from Sagan what kind of person he wanted to be.

Tyson went to Harvard and graduated with a degree in physics, then went to the University of Texas at Austin for a master's degree. He stopped before getting his doctorate and went to teach at the University of Maryland for a year before going to Columbia University, where he received his doctorate in 1991. He started to work for the Hayden Planetarium in 1994.

In 2001 President Bush appointed Tyson to a commission to study and report on the future of the aerospace industry. He and the other scientists published a report that described how the United States could build a successful future for transportation, space exploration, and national security. In 2004 Bush appointed Tyson to another important committee, officially called the committee for Implementation of the United States Space Exploration Policy, but nicknamed the Moon, Mars, and Beyond Commission.

That same year, NASA awarded Tyson its Distinguished Public Service Medal, the highest award it can give to someone who is not a government employee. It was also the year he hosted his first television show, *Origins*, as part of PBS's *Nova* series. *Origins* is about how the universe and the planet Earth developed. In 2006 the head of NASA invited Tyson to join its Advisory Council, which helps NASA decide its priorities.

Tyson has hosted very famous television programs, especially the 2014 reboot of *Cosmos*, originally hosted by Carl Sagan, who was the most famous American astronomer during his lifetime. Tyson's reboot of *Cosmos* won four Emmy Awards, a Peabody Award, and two Critics Choice awards. The National Geographic channels showed it in 181 countries in 45 languages.

THE
WARRIORS

TUSKEGEE AIRMEN

In 1938 President Roosevelt knew the United States would need military pilots for World War II and proposed legislation for the Civilian Pilot Training (CPT) Program. In Congress, Representative Everett Dirksen added a provision requiring that it be open to people of all races. The next year, the Civil Aeronautics Authority announced that it would begin training "colored people" (which was the preferred term at the time) as mechanics, pilots, and ground crew.

This photo shows the first group of Black cadets to earn their wings at Tuskegee Army Air Field in 1941. Benjamin O. Davis is in the middle.
Photo source: Smithsonian Institution

Tuskegee Institute opened its first class of thirteen cadets on July 19, 1941. Training included topics like math; Morse Code; identification of allied and enemy ships, airplanes, and submarines; meteorology (weather and how it affects flying); navigation; and instruments. Pilot training started with mechanics to help pilots understand how their planes worked and to be able to perform some maintenance and repairs if needed.

In the late 1930s, Lt. Col. Noel F. Parrish recognized the value of training Black pilots, and he befriended Cornelius Coffey. He was put in charge of the Tuskegee program and served as the base commander from 1942 to 1946. The Airmen appreciated that he treated them as fairly as possible, even though the military as a whole was segregated, and there were unfair different standards within the military. The local communities were heavily segregated and prejudiced as well; one laundromat was willing to wash clothes for captured German soldiers but not for the Tuskegee Airmen.

One of those first thirteen cadets was Capt. Benjamin O. Davis Jr. He had graduated from the United States Military Academy in 1936, the first Black graduate there in the twentieth century. His white classmates resented him, and many agreed never to speak to or even look at him except when performing official duties, and he had to eat alone. As you will see in the section about him, he became the first Black general in the military.

Many of the Airmen felt similarly isolated in the military and called themselves "the lonely eagles" because no matter how well they flew, most people didn't really accept them as part of the military.

The Tuskegee Airmen were one of the most effective units in the war. They rarely lost the bombers that they escorted and successfully fulfilled combat and bombing missions. Collectively, they earned almost 1,500 medals, despite the prejudice against them and unfair standards.

Photo source: United States Air Force
Four "red tail" planes in flight

The Airmen's incredible war records were among the biggest factors in desegregating the United States military and the fight against segregation in general. They proved again and again that race has nothing to do with talent and that there was nothing that Black people couldn't do.

A restored "red tail" plane in flight
Photo source: United States Air Force

The first Tuskegee pilots to earn their wings for the military were Second Lieutenants Lemuel R. Curtis, Charles DeBow, Mac Ross, George Spencer Roberts, and Captain Benjamin O. Davis Jr.. You can see the list of all the Tuskegee pilots at www.tuskegee.edu/support-tu/tuskegee-airmen/tuskegee-airmen-pilot-listing.

In 1949 the Air Force held their first Top Gun competition among the highest-scoring fighter pilots. The Tuskegee Airmen sent four pilots from the 332nd Fighter Group. Even though they were flying planes that were obsolete (technologically behind the times), they won the Conventional Class meet and nearly won the individual award. However, while their scores were the highest, during the middle of one of the target shooting rounds, one of the competing pilots had to change planes. That pilot's scores suddenly improved enough to beat the Tuskegee Airmen, and it seemed very likely that when the pilot got the new plane, he also got additional bullets, with more chances to hit the targets. Still, the Tuskegee Airmen won the overall award.

Lt. James Harvey, who was one of the four pilots who won the Top Gun competition, wears a hat saying, "1st Top Gun, P-47, Winner 1949." He wears it to remind people that the Tuskegee Airmen won the first competition, even if the Air Force didn't want to acknowledge it at first.

Photo credit: United States Air Force

The Air Force, though, was not willing to admit their victory. It did not print the names of the Tuskegee Airmen in the annual list of winners until 1993. Their Top Gun trophy was lost in storage at the Wright Patterson Air Force Base in Ohio for more than 55 years until 2004. However, Zellie Rainey Orr, a researcher and historian, knew it had to be somewhere. She called and emailed the Air Force to urge them to find it because it is such an important piece of aviation history. They found it five days later, and it is now on display at the base.

Casey Grant, author of this book, says, "I was lucky to know one of the Tuskegee Airmen, Chief Master Sgt. (retired) Richard Hall Jr. . He and my father, also an Air Force man, became good friends, and my childhood friends Janice White and Gerri Rogers and I affectionately called him Pops."

He was born in Winter Park, Florida, and served proudly as one of the Tuskegee Airmen. He also served in the Korean and Vietnam Wars.

Photo source: Casey Grant's personal collection

Hall grew up in Florida and went to college at Xavier University in Louisiana when he was drafted. He trained in weaponry and aircraft maintenance. He joined the 332nd Fighter Group and was a mechanic at Ramitelli Airfield in Italy.

After the war, he was stationed with the rest of the 332nd Fighter Wing at Lockbourne Air Force Base, now Rickenbacker Air National Guard Base. Benjamin O. Davis was the commanding officer.

Even though the Air Force was integrated in 1948, Hall and his unit still faced prejudice. Once when his unit was flying from South Carolina to the Gulf of Mexico, they had to change their route.

He retired in 1973. He was one of the proud Tuskegee Airmen at a ceremony in 2007 when President George W. Bush awarded them the Congressional Gold Medal.

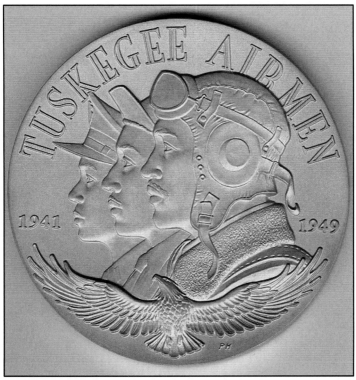

Photo source: National Museum of African American History and Culture
The Congressional Gold Medal awarded to the Tuskegee Airmen in 2007

In 2015 in his home city of Winter Garden, Florida, at the Hannibal Square Heritage Center, there is a statue of Hall to honor his courage and service to his country.

TUSKEGEE AIRWOMEN

Women also trained as mechanics, pilots, control tower operators, aircraft fuselage technicians, secretaries, and clerks at Tuskegee, and others, such as nurses, trained elsewhere but came to Tuskegee to serve. The government officially considers anybody who served at Tuskegee, male or female, military or civilian, to be among the original Tuskegee airmen.

P. H. Polk, one of the first nationally-known Black photographers,
took this photo of Tuskegee Airwomen.
Photo course: United States Army

Mildred Hemmons Carter (1921-2011) earned a business degree from Tuskegee when she was only nineteen years old. She was in the first class in the Civilian Pilot Training Program (the program later excluded women), earned her private pilot's license in 1941, and was the first civilian that the Army Air Corps hired. She literally cleared the ground for the Tuskegee Airport, bulldozing land to prepare airstrips.

During the war, she applied to become a Women's Airforce Service Pilot (WASP), one of the women pilots to fly planes domestically (within the country) to whatever base needed planes, but they turned her down because of her race. She stayed at Tuskegee and did whatever needed to be done, from administrative work to making parachutes. She taught and mentored other Black women to become pilots. In February 2011, she was officially designated a WASP.

Photo source: National Park Service. Mildred Hemmons Carter

AMELIA JONES

Amelia Jones joined the Women's Army Auxiliary Corps and worked for the 99th Pursuit Squadron for two years as an administrator, but like many other women, her service was not acknowledged until many years later.

Jones visited a program in Washington D.C., honoring the Tuskegee Airmen and told John McCaskill, who was staffing the program, about her experiences. He then helped her to get the official red jacket and other recognition of her service.

John McCaskill and Amelia Jones
Photo source: United States Park Service

BENJAMIN O. DAVIS JR.

Captain Benjamin O. Davis Jr. (1912-2002) was a United States Air Force general and commander of the World War ll Tuskegee Airmen and the first Black brigadier general in the United States Air Force.

Photo source: United States Air Force

Like many of the Black pioneers in aviation, Davis was first exposed to flight at an airshow. When he was thirteen, he took his first flight and dreamed of being a pilot. He entered the United States Military Academy at West Point in 1932. During his four years there, he faced racially isolation. His white classmates resented him, and many agreed never to speak to or even look at him except when performing official duties, and he had to eat alone. During the early part of his military career, his superiors made sure that they never put him in a position of command over white troops.

Davis was one of the original Black airmen at Tuskegee and earned his wings (meaning he qualified as a pilot) in 1942 and became one of five Black officers to complete the course. Later, he received a promotion to lieutenant colonel and became commander of the first all-Black air unit, the 99th Pursuit Squadron which was stationed in Tunisia, North Africa, in 1943.

Later that year, he returned to assume command of another squadron, the 332nd Fighter Group. During that time, some high-ranking military members, still opposed to having Black pilots, recommended disbanding them. Davis successfully argued at the hearings that the Tuskegee Airmen were among the best that the United States had trained, and so he saved the program.

In 1948 President Harry S. Truman signed an Executive Order mandating the racial integration of the armed forces. Colonel Davis helped draft the Air Force plan for implementing the order. The Air Force became the first of the services to integrate fully. Davis retired in 1970, and in 1998, he received a promotion to general, U.S. Air Force (retired). He was the first Black brigadier general in the United States Air Force.

In 1995 Davis was inducted into the International Air & Space Hall of Fame at the San Diego Air & Space Museum. Twenty years later, West Point named a barracks after him, honoring the student who had not been allowed to room with other members of his class.

BOBBY WILKS

Bobby Wilks (1931-2009) was the first Black Coast Guard aviator, the first to become a Coast Guard captain, and the first to become the commanding officer (CO) of a Coast Guard Air Station when he became CO of the Brooklyn Air Station in 1982.

Photo source: United States Coast Guard

As a young boy, he loved model airplanes, and as a young man, he even earned money by building them for a store owner. He dreamed about becoming a pilot. However, he also loved the idea of being a teacher and decided at first to follow that as his career.

Wilks attended Stowe Teachers College (now Harris-Stowe State University) in his native St. Louis, Missouri, and then joined the Naval Academy before returning to finish his degree in education. After he got his Master's in Education from St. Louis University, he joined the Coast Guard and became an aviator. Throughout his career, he learned to fly more than twenty different types of aircraft, including helicopters.

In 1963 Wilks performed a very dangerous mission to rescue a sailor who needed immediate surgery to save his life. He was supposed to land a plane on the ship to pick up the sailor, but the weather was so stormy he could not land his plane safely. After thinking over the best way to do it, Wilks performed a very risky maneuver that could have killed him, but he succeeded in rescuing the sailor.

Wilks participated in many water search and rescue missions and received the Air Medal award in 1971 for another daring rescue. This time flying a helicopter, he fought gale-force winds and a choppy sea to evacuate a critically ill sailor from a Russian vessel. He also received the Helicopter Rescue Award twice for other rescue missions.

THERESA CLAIRBORNE

Theresa Clairborne, unlike many of the pioneers featured here, didn't even think of flying as a career until she entered the Air Force ROTC program and attended the University of California. Nonetheless, she became the first Black female pilot in the United States Air Force.

Photo source: United States Air Force

As part of her training, she was required to take a flying course, and that sparked her interest in becoming a pilot. She worked to meet the requirements of the pilot training program and successfully graduated.

After leaving active service in the Air Force, Clairborne wanted to become a commercial pilot. At the time, many airlines were looking for qualified Black and female pilots. However, United Airlines had a policy that pilots had to be at least 5'4" tall, and Clairborne was shorter than that. Still, she showed that she could do everything that she needed to do as a pilot, and so United dropped the height requirement.

Clairborne started as an engineer and eventually received a promotion to captain. She is one of a few Black female captains for commercial airlines. Because she wanted to help other Black women take up aviation as a career, she helped found Sisters in the Skies.

PATRICE CLARKE
WASHINGTON

Patrice Clarke Washington (1961-), the first Black captain for a commercial airline, grew up in the Bahamas, wanting to see the world. At a high school career fair, she learned about aviation careers. She first considered being a flight attendant but then decided to be a pilot.

Photo source: UPS

She was the first African American to attend Embry-Riddle Aeronautical University and earn a bachelor's degree in aeronautical science as well as her pilot's license. Washington first flew for a Trans

Island Airways, a small charter airline in the Bahamas that flew people mostly from island to island. She flew very small planes, usually ones that could seat only six or ten passengers.

After a while, though, she wanted to fly bigger planes and spend more time in the United States. In 1984 she joined Bahamasair where she could fly bigger planes, like Boeing 737s, and fly between the Bahamas and the United States. She saw parts of the country that she had only dreamed of seeing, like the glaciers in Alaska. In 1988 UPS hired her, first as a mechanic and later promoted to pilot, and she flew huge DC-8 planes. She became a captain in 1994, the first African American captain for a commercial airline and possibly the first Black captain in the world. The same year, she married Ray Washington, a pilot who flew for American Airlines.

In an interview, Patrice Washington said, "My point of view has always been that if there's something you want to do, go ahead and do it. I've always been pretty well focused and once I decided on something, I did it."

SHAWNA ROCHELLE
KIMBRELL

Shawna Kimbrell is a lieutenant colonel in the United States Air Force and the first female African American fighter pilot in the history of the Air Force. Her parents were immigrants from Ghana who became United States citizens and encouraged their children to pursue their dreams through education.

In an interview, Kimbrell once said, "(Education) was the thing that opened doors. If you got your education, you could do whatever you wanted to do. That was how our house was run."

When Kimbrell was in the fourth grade, she knew she wanted to be a fighter pilot. She had her first flying lesson when she was fourteen years old. She earned her pilot's license and joined the Civil Air Patrol, a government-run nonprofit that teaches young people how to fly. It also helps people during natural disasters and other emergencies, and she runs search and rescue operations.

Photo source: United States Air Force

Kimbrell enrolled in the U.S. Air Force Academy in Colorado and graduated in 1998 with a Bachelor of Science in General Engineering. She then went on to pilot training at Laughlin Air Force Base in Texas and earned her pilot's wings in 1999. Later that year, she enrolled in Fighter Fundamental training at Randolph Air Force Base, and in August 2020, she became the first African American female fighter pilot in the USAF.

The training was very difficult, and in an interview she commented, "There were times when I didn't think that I was going to make it through. It was in those times I learned to be humble and realize there is a point in everyone's struggle — no matter how strong they are — when they need help, and the key is to seek it out before it is too late." Her persistence and willingness to seek help when she needed it paid off.

BRENDA ROBINSON

Brenda Robinson (1956-) was the first Black female pilot for the United States Navy, and later she became the first female African American pilot for American Airlines. She liked the idea of airplanes and flying even when she was young, even though some people told her that as a girl, she could only be a flight attendant. Still, when she attended a career program, she decided she would like to work in aviation as an air traffic controller.

Photo source: United States Navy

After she graduated from high school, she went to Dowling College in New York, one of the best aviation schools on the East Coast. She was the first Black woman to study there. Soon after, she decided to go back to her first dream of being a pilot, not an air traffic controller. While she attended college, she also received her private pilot's certificate. She graduated with a degree in aeronautics and started the Navy Aviation Officer Candidate School in 1977. This was only the second year that the Navy admitted women, and it picked only ten women for that year. This made her feel proud but also aware that if she made mistakes, people would think that Black women could not handle flying for the military.

In 1980 she became the first African American woman in the U.S. Navy to earn her wings. During her later career, she achieved the position of lieutenant commander and served as a Navy instructor, evaluator, and VIP transport pilot, piloting major military figures and even some celebrities.

In 1992 she transferred to the Naval Reserves (meaning that she no longer worked full time for the Navy but would be available in an emergency) and started to work for American Airlines. After she retired, she started a second career teaching young people about flying and even founded a camp, Aviation Camps of the Carolinas, to teach teens about aviation. In 1995 she wrote a book, *Success is an Attitude: Goal Achievement for a Lifetime.*

THE
FLIGHT CREWS
AND
GROUND STAFF

RUTH CAROL TAYLOR

Ruth Carol Taylor (1931-) first worked as a nurse and then for the New York Transit Authority. She thought that it was unfair that Black women were not being hired as flight attendants (or stewardesses, as they were called then), and she decided to break the racial barrier.

Photo source: Unknown

She first applied at TWA, but they rejected her. After she heard that Mohawk, a small regional airline, was looking for Black candidates, she successfully applied. Her first flight was on February 11, 1958. However, like teachers, stewardesses were supposed to be single, and she lost her job six months later when she married. Ironically, she traveled more after she left the travel industry, and when she was living in Barbados, she started its first journal for nurses.

She returned to New York where she co-founded the Institute for Inter Racial Harmony in 1982. Fifty years after she broke that racial barrier, the New York State Assembly officially recognized her for her accomplishment as the first African American flight attendant.

The very first Black flight attendant in the world was Léopoldine Doualla-Bell Smith (1939-). Smith was born in Cameroon to the royal Douala family of Cameroon, making her not just the first Black stewardess (as flight attendants were called then) but the first royal stewardess.

While she was attending high school, Air France offered Smith a job as a "ground hostess," a kind of hospitality and operations manager's job. She did so well that she went to France for more training and started to work for another French airline, Union Aéromaritime de Transport, which was expanding its operations in Africa. She flew her first flight in 1957. She did not know it then, but she was making history as the first Black flight attendant.

She flew for twelve years, became manager of a travel agency based in Gabon, and then decided to study English at Georgetown University in Washington D.C. There, she met and married Leroy Smith, an American. Smith returned to Gabon in 1976 and took a management role at the Libreville Airport. She actively promoted travel and tourism in Africa and played a major role in developing its travel sector, which created jobs and educated people around the world about Africa and African cultures.

In 1983 Smith and her husband joined the Peace Corps and went to Peru. When they retired, they moved to Denver, Colorado, where they formed Business and Intercultural Services for Educational Travel and Associated Learning (BISETAL).

Léopoldine Doualla-Bell Smith
Photo source: Source unknown

PATRICIA BANKS EDMISTON

Patricia Banks Edmiston (1937-) applied to and gained acceptance at Grace Downs Air Career School in New York City. She graduated with excellent grades and applied for flight attendant positions with Trans World Airlines, Mohawk Airlines, and Capital Airlines.

Photo source: Personal collection of Patricia Banks-Edmiston.
Used with permission

After Capital Airlines rejected her for a job, one of the people charged with hiring decisions said that they had rejected her because the airline "didn't hire negroes." Edmiston decided to fight this, and she filed a complaint against Capital Airlines with the New York State Commission Against Discrimination in 1956.

Edmiston won the case in 1960 when the Commission ruled in her favor and ordered Capital Airlines to hire her within thirty days. If it did not do so, they would take the case to the United States Supreme Court.

Edmiston completed Capital Airlines stewardess training and then became the first African American stewardess to work for a commercial airline. She flew only for a year before deciding to return to school to pursue her college education.

Edmiston served on the board of directors of Black Flight Attendants of America, Inc., and was inducted into the Black Aviation Hall of Fame at the National Civil Rights Museum in Memphis, Tennessee, in August 2010. She is retired and stays active, practicing Shotokan martial arts, in which she holds a black belt.

OSCAR WAYMAN HOLMES

Oscar Wayman Holmes (1916-2001) was the first Black pilot in the United States Navy and the first Black air traffic controller. While he always wanted to fly, he decided that he should pick something where he would be more likely to get a job, and so, he earned a Bachelor's and Master's in Chemistry.

Photo source: United States Navy

After teaching chemistry and then working as a chemist, he saw in a newspaper that the Civilian Pilot Training Program (CPTP), which the government had established to train pilots for WWII, was holding an examination to win scholarships to study aviation. Holmes applied, won a scholarship, and received training to earn a private pilot's license. His first assignment to the New York airway traffic control center was as an assistant controller, making him the first Black air traffic controller. He was very light-skinned, and all of his supervisors thought that he was white. Holmes never claimed to be white, but knowing the advantages of passing as white, he never said that he was Black.

However, when he went through the program and became an air traffic controller, one of his supervisors recommended him for a promotion. On the paperwork, Holmes filled out his race as Negro. Upper management noted on his application not to accept it. Recognizing that he could not be promoted as an air traffic controller because of his race, Holmes saw an announcement in the paper that the Navy was recruiting pilots. He applied – without mentioning his race – and became commissioned as an ensign pilot in 1942. Not until he had to submit a copy of his birth certificate did the Navy realize that they had commissioned a Black pilot and Black officer.

He completed flight instructor training, but the Navy did not promote him to teach the same way that they promoted the white men in his class. Instead, they sent him to interview potential cadet recruits. He formally requested to be assigned to flight training or work as an aircraft delivery pilot, and in 1944 he was assigned to fly aircraft to their destinations. Though other African Americans served in segregated units, Holmes, because he looked white, was able to serve alongside other white officers. He did not tell people that he was black, especially because so many of his routes took him through the Deep

South, where he would be in danger if people knew he was sharing work, meals, and sleeping quarters with white officers.

In 1946 he returned to work as an air traffic controller and finally received the promotion he had earned previously. He remained an air traffic controller until he retired.

ELEANOR WILLIAMS

Eleanor Williams was the first Black woman to become an air traffic controller in 1971. Air traffic controllers, as the title implies, direct air traffic to make sure that pilots always keep a safe distance from other planes. Being an air traffic controller is hard work because they have to be very focused at all times, but it pays well. Most air traffic controllers earn at least $120,000. Learn more about becoming an air traffic controller from the Bureau of Labor Statistics here: https://www.bls.gov/ooh/transportation-and-material-moving/air-traffic-controllers.htm

Photo source: FAA

Williams excelled in high school and received a four-year college scholarship, but she attended only one semester, dropping out to get married and have children. She later commented, "I got married and started having my kids too fast."

She and her family moved to Anchorage, Alaska, where her sister owned a janitorial services company. Unable to find another job without a college degree, she started working as a janitor and cleaned the offices at the Federal Aviation Administration, the government organization that regulates all non-military aviation. While she regretted dropping out of college, she decided not to give up on getting an education and a career she would love.

Williams took free classes at the local community college to train as a secretary. She got the job she wanted at the FAA and started working to earn promotions. She took the air traffic control exam, passed it, and started training in 1968. She received certification in 1971, and the Anchorage Air Traffic Control Center hired her. She did not learn until 1980 that she was the first African American woman to receive certification as an air traffic controller.

Williams continued to earn promotions and traveled across the United States, eventually rising to become manager of the Cleveland area control center, which became the busiest in the country while she was managing it. She became a goodwill ambassador for the FAA, teaching people about careers as air traffic controllers.

❧ THE INVENTORS ❧

We would not have transportation or aviation as we know them today if it weren't for some African American inventors. There are many important inventors, but you will recognize the work of some of them if you have ever used a call button on a plane, received directions on a cell phone, looked at photos of the moon's surface, or used a Super Soaker.

MIRIAM E. BENJAMIN

Miriam E. Benjamin (1861-1947) was from Charleston, South Carolina. One of her inventions is still in use today on airplanes and is an important part of the passenger experience.

Photo source: Unknown

She first worked as a school teacher but studied inventing on the side. In 1888 she received a patent for what she called the "Gong and Signal Chair" for hotels and restaurants. This made her the second African American woman to receive a patent. Hotel and restaurant dining rooms could not always tell who needed service when or who wanted to be left alone. Hotels and private clubs also used to have reading rooms where members or guests could relax and read. If they wanted something from the staff, they had to clap their hands or shout, which made it difficult for staff to tell who called; it was also noisy for the other guests.

Benjamin designed a chair equipped with a gong and a small button on the back of the chair that lit up, so the attendant could tell who needed service.

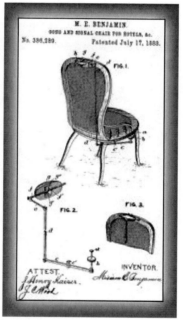

Photo source: United States Patent Office

Benjamin went to college at Howard University in Washington D.C. Howard was one of the few universities to accept Black people at the time, and today it is still one of the most prestigious among Historically Black Colleges and Universities. She first studied medicine, but she realized that her real love was law and patents, so she earned a law degree and worked on patent law for the rest of her life.

GLADYS WEST

While we think of scientific discovery and inventions as creating something new, most discoveries and inventions are based on a foundation of previous work that made them possible. Dr. Gladys West's (1930-) discoveries led to the development of the Global Positioning System (GPS). This is the technology that gets information from satellites to locate where you are and give you directions in real time. Every time you get directions on your phone, it is because of her work. She was not part of the same group of "Hidden Figures" that enabled the United States to send humans into outer space, but she performed the same types of calculations.

Dr. Gladys B. West
Photo source: United States Air Force

West grew up in poverty, but "I realized I had to get an education to get out." She worked hard in school and went to college at Virginia State University (then Virginia State College), graduating at the top of her class.

In 1956 she started to work for the Naval Surface Warfare Center – Dahlgren Division. She was the second Black woman ever to work there and one of only four Black people. She collected data from satellites, which then was a very new technology, and her approaches to the data led to the development of the Global Positioning System, now known as GPS.

The Air Force Space and Missile Pioneers Hall of Fame inducted her in 2018.

GEORGE ROBERT CARRUTHERS

Katherine Johnson and more "Hidden Figures" made it possible for humans to go to the moon. George Robert Carruthers (1939-2020) invented the camera that the astronauts took with them.

Carruthers is holding one of the films that the astronauts brought back with them.
Photo source: NASA

His father was a civil engineer at Wright Patterson Air Force Base, but the family moved to a farm when Carruthers was young. When he was a boy, he loved reading about space and even built a telescope when he was ten years old.

His family moved to Chicago, and Carruthers often visited the Adler Planetarium and looked at the skies through their telescopes. He went to the University of Illinois and studied aerospace and engineering. He earned a doctorate in aeronautical and astronautical engineering in late 1964 and went to work for the Naval Research Laboratory.

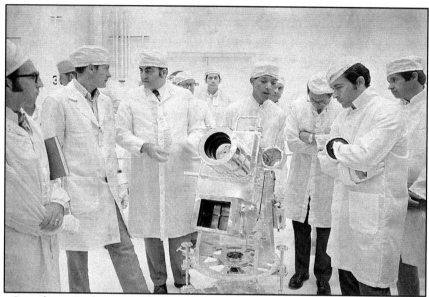

Carruthers is in the center. The two people on his left are Lunar Module Pilot Charles Duke and Rocco Petrone, Apollo program director, and the person on his right is Apollo 16 Commander John Young.
Photo source: NASA

The astronauts going to Mars needed a camera that would be lightweight, easy to use, and reliable, and of course take excellent pictures. Carruthers designed a camera that was just what they needed. After the astronauts returned from the moon, Carruthers kept creating new developments for cameras and also started several education programs to encourage young people to consider science and technology careers. In 2013 President Barack Obama awarded Carruthers the 2011 National Medal for Technology and Innovation.

https://airandspace.si.edu/stories/editorial/george-carruthers-astronautical-engineer-astronomer

LONNIE JOHNSON

Lonnie Johnson (1949-) invented one of the most famous and best-selling toys of all time, the Super Soaker. He was also a NASA engineer for more than ten years and before that, an Air Force engineer.

Photo course: Office of Naval Research

Johnson started inventing things when he was a child, and when he was in high school, he won first prize at a science fair in 1968 with a robot that he had invented. One of his heroes was George Washington Carver, the Black inventor who revolutionized agriculture in the southern United States.

Johnson went to Tuskegee and earned a Bachelor's in Mechanical Engineering and a Master's in Nuclear Engineering before joining the Air Force as an engineer. He led several important projects there, including the nuclear power source for the Galileo mission to send a spacecraft to Jupiter.

He originated the idea for the Super Soaker while trying to think of a better way to cool heat pumps. One of his experiments with a different kind of nozzle blasted water across the room, and he realized it would make a fun toy. Since his original invention, the Super Soaker has had almost $1 billion in sales.

Johnson has worked on many important inventions and founded Johnson Research & Development to develop even more. One of the most important projects that he is working on is the Johnson Thermoelectric Energy Converter (JTEC). Johnson cares very much about developing renewable energy, and he designed an engine to convert heat directly into electricity, which would make solar power much cheaper and easier to provide.

THE SPOLIGHT ON DELTA

Because I spent my entire flying career at Delta, I came to know and make friends with some of their pioneers. Here are a few with their stories.

PATRICIA GRACE MURPHY

Patricia Grace Murphy was the first Black flight attendant for Delta, and so she was a personal friend and inspiration. She originally attended Atlantic Airline School in Kansas City, Missouri, where she learned how to become a ticket agent. Back then, ticketing was very complicated, and an agent had to learn and memorize a lot of facts, including airline codes for every city with an airport. She then decided that she wanted to be a flight attendant and see all the places she had learned about in school.

Photo source: Patricia Grace Murphy's collection. Used by permission.

Like many Black stewardesses, including me, she had a difficult time finding an apartment near an airport because many people didn't want to rent to Black people. She also faced prejudice from passengers, including ones who wouldn't let her serve them. Murphy refused to let this stop her. "I wanted to get out and spread my wings," she said about her dream.

STEPHANIE JOHNSON

Stephanie Johnson thought about becoming a pilot or following some other aviation career when she was a young girl, but she didn't plan on it as a career. When she was in high school, her physics teacher took her and some other students for a flight which rekindled her dream.

Photo source: Delta Airlines

With a lot of encouragement from her teachers, family, and friends, Johnson went to Kent State University to study aviation. She was the first person in her family to graduate from college, so this was a real source of pride for them. With a degree in aerospace technology, she became a flight instructor for Kent State's aviation program.

Johnson's first airline job was with Mesa Airlines. In 1997 she became the first Black female pilot for Northwest Airlines. There were only twelve other Black female pilots flying for major airlines. In 2008 Northwest merged with Delta, and in 2016, Johnson became the first Black female captain to fly for Delta. During her first year as captain, she made Delta Air Lines history again when she captained a flight from Detroit to Las Vegas with First Officer Dawn Cook, another African American, on the first African American-led flight, a first for Delta. In 2019 Captain Johnson assumed an additional role and became the first woman to hold Chief Pilot position for Delta.

A director of the Cleveland Aviation Career Education Academy, she believes strongly in aviation as a career. She also participates in the Detroit Aviation Career Education Academy which teaches high school students about aviation.

Photo source: Delta Airlines
Stephanie Johnson and Dawn Cook

Rachelle Jones, Stephanie Grant, Diana Galloway, and Robin Rogers were the first all-Black female flight crew on a commercial flight in the United States. On February 12, 2009, they served on Atlantic Southeast Airlines, a historic flight for its code share airline, Delta Flight 5202, from Atlanta, Georgia, to Nashville, Tennessee.

SAM GRADDY

Samuel L. Graddy was the first African American pilot for Delta. When asked when he became interested in flying, he answered, "I've never been interested in anything other than flying."

Photo: Delta collection

JOHN BAILEY

John Bailey was born on March 31, 1945, in Coalwood, West Virginia, and grew up in Buffalo, New York. As a child, Bailey loved flying so much that he covered the ceiling of his bedroom with model airplanes suspended by his mother's sewing thread.

Photo source: John Bailey's personal collection

Following college, he joined the U.S. Air Force with the hopes of one day becoming an Air Force pilot. Unfortunately, prior to entering the Air Force, he was informed by the medical technician that he had sickle cell anemia, therefore disqualifying him from flying. As a result, Bailey entered the Air Force as a non-flying logistics officer which required that he provide personnel and supplies to Bomb Wings involving aircraft support for pilots, aircraft, maintenance personnel, and supply personnel throughout the entire world.

Fortunately, after Bailey's commanding officer read his medical report, he inquired what had happened and why he was not on flight status. He then commanded the flight surgeon to give Bailey a thorough examination, including numerous blood tests. Following the examination, doctors determined that Bailey did not have sickle cell anemia, and he was immediately authorized to attend USAF Undergraduate Pilot Training.

During Bailey's time in the Air Force, he flew more than 141 combat missions over Southeast Asia and received the Distinguished Flying Cross DFC. This medal is "awarded to any person who has distinguished themselves by single acts of heroism or extraordinary achievement while participating in aerial flight."

After leaving the Air Force, Bailey applied to the commercial airlines, but at that time, they had very few Black pilots. The first one hired was in 1965, when Continental Airlines hired Marlon Green. Subsequently, in 1968 Delta Air Lines hired Sam Graddy.

In 1972 immediately upon his retirement from the military, Bailey called Graddy to ask if he should accept a job offer from Delta. Graddy encouraged him to do so, and Bailey became a Delta pilot in 1973. Thirty-one years later, Bailey retired from Delta Air Lines.

EUGENE HARMOND

For most of aviation history, flight attendants have been women, and the job became stereotyped, like nursing or teaching preschool, as something that interested only women. In 1973 Eugene Harmond helped to change that.

Photo source: Author's collection, used with permission

He felt inspired to apply for a job as a flight attendant back in the early 1970s after a guest at one of his parties complimented him on his fine hosting skills and suggested that he become a flight attendant. Back then, flying was much more luxurious and expensive, with much more personal service from the attendants for all classes. Harmond thought this would be a good way to see the world, and so he applied for a job. Delta Air Lines hired him in 1973.

Harmond faced discrimination in many ways. The airlines always arranged and paid in advance for hotel rooms for their flight attendants, but one hotel in New York City refused to honor Harmond's reservation. He rode around in a cab all that night because he couldn't find any hotels that would let him stay. Eugene is still flying in 2021, with almost fifty years of service to his credit.

ORGANIZATIONS AND ASSOCIATIONS

Americans have always known that no one can accomplish everything on their own. Some of the biggest changes in the United States – the American Revolution, the abolitionist movement to end slavery, the fight for women's rights, and the Civil Rights struggle – began with people coming together in associations and organizations. Many of the people in this book founded or helped associations to assist others to reach the skies. Here is a list of associations that are active today and in-depth profiles of some of the most influential ones.

The Organization of Black Aerospace Professionals offers educational programs and scholarships. www.obap.org

The Black Aviation Airline Pioneers works to promote the contributions of Blacks to aviation and to encourage Black youth and adults to consider airline careers. www.baap.info

Sisters of the Skies offers scholarships and mentorships to Black women pilots. www.sistersoftheskies

Bessie Coleman Aviation All-Stars introduces students to various careers in aviation and explores aviation history. www.bessiecolemanaviationallstars.org

Aviation Camps of the Carolinas is a one-day experience at airports that introduces young people to aviation careers as mechanics, pilots, air traffic controllers, and similar opportunities. Brenda Robinson founded these camps. www.aviationcamps.org

Black Flight Attendants of America, Inc. was founded to help support and provide a community for Black flight attendants. www.blackflightattendantsofamerica.org

ORGANIZATION OF BLACK AIRLINE PILOT, INC. - OBAP BEN THOMAS

In 1976 Ben Thomas, then a pilot for Eastern Airlines, wanted to address discrimination in aviation and encourage people of color to pursue careers in aviation. He invited thirty-seven Black pilots to meet in Chicago and discuss how to do this. Together, they formed the Organization of Black Airline Pilots, now called the Organization of Black Aerospace Professionals.

Photo source: OBAP

OBAP is active in political advocacy; that is, they gather information about important topics and talk to political officials about those topics. In 1982, for example, they warned the United States Air Force that soon there would be a greater demand for military pilots and that there would not be enough unless the Air Force started recruiting young Black people to become pilots.

In 1992 in coordination with the FAA, OBAP started Aerospace Career Education (ACE) Academies to help teach students about careers in aviation and aerospace, and in 2005, OBAP started another program called Aerospace Professionals in Schools to introduce students to Black leaders in aerospace and encourage them to consider aviation careers.

One of the founding members of OBAP was Captain John M. Bailey Jr. After retiring from his job as a pilot for Delta Air Lines, he founded a speakers' group, Black Aviation Airline Pioneers, to "maintain fraternal relationships between aviation pioneers from years past, and to encourage minorities and women to seek career opportunities in aviation."

BLACK FLIGHT ATTENDANTS OF AMERICA, INC. (BFAOA, INC.) JACQUELINE JACQUET-WILIAMS

Jacqueline Jacquet-Williams was a flight attendant who frequently experienced discrimination from passengers and sometimes from colleagues. She was often the only person of color on her team which sometimes made her feel isolated.

Photo source: Jacqueline Jacquet-Williams

To make sure that no Black flight attendant would feel like they were alone, she founded a nonprofit organization called Black Flight Attendants of America, Inc. (BFAOA, Inc) in 1974. Its goal was to promote and foster racial ethnic diversity and necessary skills to compete in the aviation industry by expanding educational opportunities through travel for underprivileged communities across the country, "promoting the legacy of black history in aviation globally."

BFAOA helps African Americans to become flight attendants by giving scholarships and helping its members find ways to volunteer to help others. The organization also has worked with the Organization of Black Aerospace Professionals (OBAP) as well as Aviation Career Education (ACE) camps and Boy Scouts events. This is part of a long tradition of African Americans forming clubs and associations to help one another and smooth the path for the next generations.

THE EARLIEST AFRICAN AMERICAN FLIGHT ATTENDANTS

American Airlines: Joan Dorsey

Capital Airlines: Patricia Banks-Edmiston

Continental Airlines: Diane Hunter

Delta Air Lines: Patricia Grace Murphy

Mohawk: Ruth Carol Taylor

National Airlines: Undra Mays

Pan American World Airways: PAN AM: Sheila Nutt

Trans World Airlines: Margaret Grant

INTERVIEWS WITH PIONEERS

I host a weekly podcast, "The Fly Girl Show," that features interviews with Black aviation pioneers, including some of the people featured or mentioned in this book, as well as many pioneers not included. Here are the dates the interviews aired.

www.blogtalkradio.com/theflygirl10

9/07/2014 – Patricia Grace Murphy

10/15/2014 – Eugene Harmond

1/12/2015 – John Bailey

4/08/2015 – Richard Hall

9/24/2015 – Jaqueline Jacquet-Williams

10/19/2015 – Patricia Banks Edmiston

03/08/2016 – Brenda Robinson

8/07/2017 – Guy Bluford

3//16/2017 – Stephanie Johnson

2/26/2020 – Patricia Banks Edmiston

7/05/2020 – Leopoldine Smith

1/29/21 – Leslie Irby

1/29/2021 – Richard Hall (tribute to his memory)

3/4/2021 – Zellie Rainey Orr

GLOSSARY

A lot of the words related to flying are based on the roots "aero" or "avia." That's because "aero" means "air" in Greek, and a lot of words in English, especially scientific words, originated in Greek. In Latin, the root "avia" means "bird," which inspired words related to flying.

Aeronaut: An aeronaut travels through the air with a balloon or other lighter-than-aircraft.

Aerospace: Aerospace is the technology related to aviation and outer space.

Aviation: Aviation is the making and flying airplanes.

Aviator: An aviator is the person who flies a plane.

Astronomy: Astronomy is the branch of science that studies the stars and space.

Astronaut: An astronaut is a person who travels in outer space.

Commemorative stamp: A commemorative stamp honors a person, group, or event. This is one way that governments recognize people or organizations who have contributed to their country.

Commercial airline: A commercial airline primarily carries passengers, rather than cargo. Some of the biggest commercial airlines in the United States are American, Delta, Southwest, and United.

Discrimination: Discrimination involves making unfair judgments about people based on various categories. For example, discrimination says that girls can't play certain sports.

Entrepreneur: A person who starts a new business is an entrepreneur.

Gong: A metal disk that rings when it's struck is a gong.

Global Positioning System (GPS): This is a system that locates objects like cell phones based on signals that satellites send. NASA manages these satellites and the ground receivers they need to operate.

Orbit: To orbit means to circle around something. The moon orbits the earth, and the earth orbits the sun. Space satellites also orbit the earth.

Pandemic: A pandemic is a serious disease that occurs all over the world.

Satellite: A satellite is something that orbits another thing. Satellites can be natural, like the moon, or machines, like GPS satellites.

Spacewalk: A spacewalk refers to whenever an astronaut leaves the spaceship or the space station.

Thermoelectric converter device: This kind of device changes heat into electricity. If you noticed that the word sounds kind of like "thermometer," you're right. The word "thermo" means "heat" in Greek and is also the root of the word "thermos."

Vaccine: A vaccine is a substance that protects the body from sickness by preparing the immune system to fight it. Vaccines protect people from diseases that used to kill millions.

Vaccination: Vaccination is the receiving of a vaccine.

EARLIEST BLACK PILOTS ON COMMERCIAL OR SHIPPING AIRLINES

American Airlines

First African American pilot: David Harris

First African American female pilot: Brenda Robinson

Delta Air Lines

First African American pilot: Sam Graddy

First African American female pilot: Dana Nelson

Eastern Airlines

First African American pilot: Lellie Morris

FedEx

First African American pilot – Carroll Waters

First All Black flight crew - Flying Tiger (now FedEx) Captain - George Rayner. First Officer - Frank Campbell. 2nd Officer - Fred McClurkin

New York Airways

First African American pilot to fly passengers (helicopter): Perry H. Young

Northwest Airlines

First African American pilot: Woodson M. Fountain

First female African American pilot: Stephanie Johnson

Pan American Airways (PAN AM)

First African American pilot: Perry Jones

Seaboard World

First African American pilot to fly cargo: Augustus Martin

Texas International Airlines TIA

First African American female pilot: Jill E. Brown-Hiltz

United Airlines

First African American pilot: Bill Norwood

First African American female pilot: Shirley Suber (Tyus)

Western Airlines

First African American pilot: Fred Pitch

TRIBUTE TO
ALICE COACHMAN

Alice Coachman (1923-2014) was my cousin and hero, the first Black woman to win an Olympic gold medal. She never gave up on her dream, and so I pay tribute to her in every book I write.

Photo source: The Coachman family

She was born in Albany, Georgia, the fifth of ten children. She loved sports, especially running, and she worked hard at it. But because she was Black, she couldn't go to the best track and field training facilities. She made her own training program, running barefoot on dirt roads near her home because that was the closest to running on professional tracks. She made her own equipment to practice jumping.

Coachman's family and fifth grade teacher encouraged her to join the track team in high school. She competed in high school matches and won national championships in the high jump (which she won ten years in a row from 1939 to 1948), the outdoor 50-meter dash (which she won four years in a row from 1943 to 1947), the outdoor 100-meter race, and the indoor 50-meter dash. The first time she won the high jump, she had never jumped using the official measures and equipment. She had taught herself with her own equipment, so she didn't let the new format interfere. She did her best and won.

After her first national championship, when she was sixteen, Cleve Abbott, the track and field coach at Tuskegee Institute and a former track star himself, offered her a scholarship to Tuskegee Institute's Preparatory School. The school is part of the Tuskegee Institute, home of the Tuskegee Airmen.

After finishing high school at the Preparatory School, she started at Tuskegee Institute. She graduated from Tuskegee Institute in 1946 with a degree in dressmaking. She later enrolled at Albany State College, where she received a B.S in Home Economics with a minor in science in 1949. She became a teacher and track and field instructor.

She always dreamed of winning an Olympic medal, but just when she was getting ready for the 1940 Olympics, World War II broke out, and the Olympics were cancelled. She had hoped to participate in the 1944 Olympics, but those were cancelled as well. After the war ended, Coachman tried out for the U.S. Olympics team and broke a world record in her trial when she jumped 5 feet and 4 inches. At the Olympics, she broke her own record with a jump of 5 feet, 6 and 1/8 inches. She was the first Black woman and only American woman to win an Olympic gold medal in athletics in 1948. Her medal was presented by King George VI.

On August 23, 1999, Albany, Georgia, opened a new school, the Alice Coachman Elementary School. Their motto is "Putting Children First."

Attention teachers and young readers: we have provided three quizzes to test your knowledge concerning the information contained in *Stars and Beyond: Stories of Black Heroes in Aviation.* The answer key to the quiz questions can be found following Quiz #3.

QUIZ #1

1. The Tuskegee Airmen learned to fly in _____.

2. Bessie Coleman earned her pilot's license from _____, France.

3. Leopoldine Smith was the first Black stewardess in the world and she was also a _____.

4. William J. Powell's favorite pet was a _____.

5. A _____ is a person that likes to solve mathematical problems.

6. _____ _____ was the first pilot to fly coast to coast.

7. B. Banneker built a _____ out of wood that kept accurate time.

8. Janet Bragg was the first Black female to earn a _____ pilot's license.

9. William Powell wanted to see more young Black people learn how to fly, so he wrote a book named _____ _____.

10. William Powell opened the first Black Aero Club in _____.

11. Cornelius Coffey built the first Black owned airstrip in

_____.

12. The Tuskegee Airmen painted the tail of their airplanes

_____.

13. Cornelius Coffey built the first Black owned _____ in Robbins, Illinois.

14. Bessie _____ was the first Black female to earn her pilot's license.

QUIZ #2

1. Leslie Irby had to learn how to fly a airplane with
_____ controls.

2. Eugene _____ was the first Black male flight
attendant for Delta Air Lines.

3. _____ is the activities surrounding mechanical
flight and the aircraft industry.

4. Guion Bluford was the first African American to travel to
_____.

5. Bessie _____ was the first Black female to earn her
pilot's license.

6. _____ _____ was the first Black female astronaut.

7. An _____ is a scientist that studies stars, planets,
moons and comets.

8. William _____ wanted to see more young Black
people learn how to fly so he wrote a book named *Black Wings*.

9. Patricia Banks _____ was the first Black stewardess
for a U.S commercial airline.

10. Katherine Johnson was one of the first African American women to work as a NASA _____.

11. This invention was first used on the _____ _____ in restaurants and is no used on airplanes to call a flight attendant.

12. Mildred Carter was the first _____ the Army Air Corps hired.

13. Katherine Johnson was the first _____ that helped send the first astronauts to outer space.

14. A person that travels to space is called an _____.

QUIZ #3

1. Stephanie _____ is the first Black female captain for Delta.

2. Willa _____ was the first Black women to run for the United States Congress.

3. Eugene Jacques _____ was the first Black American military pilot.

4. Casey _____ is the author of *Stars and Beyond: Stories of Black Heroes in Aviation*.

5. A person who invents, especially one who devises some new process, appliance, machine, or article is called an _____.

6. Brenda Robinson was the first black female pilot for the U.S _____.

7. Bessie Coleman was popularly known as Queen Bess and _____ _____.

8. Charles W. Chapelle excelled in different areas and was sometimes called a _____ man.

9. A _____ is a person that has a license to fly hot air balloons.

10. Patricia Grace _____ as the first Black stewardess for Delta Air Lines.

11. A person that travels to space is called an _____.

12. Miriam Benjamin was the second African American female to receive a patent. She _____ the Gong and signal chair.

13. Cornelius Coffey built the first Black owned airstrip in _____ Illinois.

14. Janet _____ was the first Black female to earn a commercial pilot's license.

ANSWERS TO QUIZ #1:

1. Alabama
2. Paris
3. Princess
4. Monkey
5. Mathematician
6. James Banning
7. Clock
8. Commercial
9. Black Wings
10. California
11. Illinois
12. Red
13. Airstrip
14. Coleman

ANSWERS TO QUIZ #2:

1. Hand
2. Harmond
3. Aviation
4. Space
5. Coleman
6. Mae Jemison
7. Astronomer
8. Powell
9. Edmiston
10. Scientist
11. Gong Chair
12. Civilian
13. Mathematician
14. Astronaut

ANSWERS TO QUIZ #3:

1. Johnson
2. Brown
3. Bullard
4. Grant
5. Invented
6. Navy
7. Brave Bessie
8. Renaissance
9. Aeronaul
10. Murphy
11. Astronaut
12. Inventor
13. Robbins.
14. Bragg

SPECIAL THANKS
TO MY SUPPORT TEAM

I would like to thank Ann Feeney for your significant contribution and editing, making it possible to turn my book into a source of education, highlighting the importance of aviation and our Black heroes in aviation to the world.

Thank you, Susan Giffin, for your friendship, editing, and formatting.

Thank you to my dear friend Captain John Bailey for always being available for any technical aviation questions.

EPOC – Empowering People of Color, my Mastermind group. Herb Henderson, Rhonda Thomas, Dr. Vincent Wiggins, Thank you for supplying direction and creative intelligence for all my projects.